Moyra Donaldson was born in Newtownards, Co. Down in 1956 and educated at Queen's University, Belfast. Her first collection, *Snakeskin Stilettos*, was published by Lagan Press in 1998. She is currently the literary editor for *Fortnight* magazine.

By the same author

Poetry
Snakeskin Stilettos

As editor
Down at the Millennium

BENEATH THE ICE

BENEATH THE ICE

MOYRA DONALDSON

LAGAN PRESS
BELFAST
2001

The publishers would like to acknowledge the following in which some of these poems, or versions of them, originally appeared: *Art Words*, *BBC Northern Ireland*, *Black Mountain Review*, *Radio Ulster*, *Fortnight*, *Poetry Ireland* and *The Works*.

The author would also like to acknowledge the Arts Council of Northern Ireland for a bursary in order to let her complete this collection and Ards Council for a bursary to enable her to attend the Tyrone Guthrie Centre.

Published by
Lagan Press
183 University Avenue
Belfast BT7 1GZ

ISBN: 1 873687 68 0
Author: Donaldson, Moyra
Title: Beneath the Ice
2001

Set in Palatino
Printed by Noel Murphy Printing, Belfast

Ring the bells that still can ring.
Forget your perfect offering.
There is a crack in everything—
That's how the light gets in.
—'Anthem', Leonard Cohen

CONTENTS

WORDS IN THE MIRROR

precious ornaments, china teacups,
doors you're not allowed to open,
cawing rooks in the tall trees,
cracks in the earth where the devil lives

                              no ice cream for you, Miss,
                              in your red coat and shoes

first step on the broad road
a baby step, a dream walk,
jewels to be dug from concrete
with a blunt knife, laburnum seeds,
sweet days that taste of bitterness

                              your breath obscures me

memory is a chained dog, howling
for a warm fireside, not the cold moon,
the sound easily leading you down
accessible paths to nights on your own
tethered to darkness
and the rain pattering
like padded feet in a ruined house
where secret things are kept,

                              behind the mirror, in drawers,
                              in rooms filled to choking
                              with cobwebs and dust

loneliness is a bungalow roof, still
visible over the mind's hedge

                              a farmhouse attic, where
                              childhood lies broken.

all have fallen short
of your perfect sadness

                              your lunatic ideas of plenty

sometimes I think I'm talking to myself

                              hold the mirror to your mouth

THE NIGHT OF MY CONCEPTION

Rosalyn Avenue is quiet, darkness
laps at the small pool of light
spilling from the window of my parents' house—
their first home together. Today
they have painted the bathroom
and a smell of paint lingers in the air.
My mother is in bed. Her stockings
drape the bedside chair and her hair is longer
than I remember it. She is listening
to the already routine sounds my father makes
as he shooshes the dog into the kitchen,
locks up for the night. His step
is quick and light along the hall
as if everything is within reach.

He undresses, slips beneath the candlewick bedspread,
then lays his arm along the curve of her hip,
his hand warm and wanting
against the cool white sheen of her skin
and she turns to him, needing love.

When he cries out his pleasure
she opens her eyes,
calls me by name—
and I am conceived inside her longing.
I will grow into the space between them.

SEEING THE DEMOLITION OF BANGOR RAILWAY STATION

I

They're knocking down my father,
that's what I surprise myself with, driving past.
The walls are coming down, the tower with the clock.
It's overdue of course, it always was a dingy place,
concrete and smelling of piss, and inside the booking office
he sat selling tickets—Belfast and back.
Daily, weekly or monthly he'd ask?
Thirty-five years on the same tracks.

He always said he could have been famous,
another Caruso, if only he'd gone to London
like the man wanted, the talent scout.
I have a photograph—choir, table of silver—
so who knows it might have been true,
either way of it he married my mother:
she's in the picture too.

II

I smell his sheepskin coat, the one he wears out on his scooter
and it's lovely, pressing your nose into it, your arms
stretched around his waist, snuggling in, his big back
keeping off the worst of the wind.

Look after me daddy.
I'm a child after your own heart.

III

Each time you abandoned me, daddy,
I followed the trail back home
until I was left with nothing but crumbs.
Half of me missing, phantom.

[16]

I did not want to be lost in the dark forest,
tangled in the hair of the skinny old witch
who eats children, feeds them sweet things,
then picks at their innocence with fingers of bone.

By the time you came looking for me
I was all gone, daddy. Licked up, swallowed down.

IV

He's leaning on the radiator beside the back door,
complaining about a pain in his arm.
No one is listening, and I'm only visiting,
it's nothing to do with me, the row that's raging,
something about his missing teeth and my brother's wedding.

He'd have looked a right sight in the photographs
if he'd lived long enough.

V

I thought that was the end of it.
The past is just what was,
nothing to understand,
no need for absolution
but always his face in the mirror,
the nose and mouth and eyes he gave to me,
the double helix of our link
and all that I inherited—

for when my heart always came back unheard,
I learnt like him, to just keep quiet,
lock up the anger and the pain.
You cannot blame the deaf and blind
because they do not see or hear,
you mustn't mind, and so
I too became a stone. The carved out

hollows of my eyes saw nothing.
My heart was granite

and this is how the change occurs,
childhood's painful metamorphosis
to some adult disfigurement.
Sins of fathers and mothers
manifest in each new generation's face.

My children make this matter.
I do not want to turn
a face of stone to their soft need
or crack their belief with ignorance.
My maimed best is not enough
but I can learn a different love.

Why didn't you look after me, daddy
look after yourself. Daddy
there is nothing that cannot be rebuilt.

MY MOTHER COMES TO ME IN DREAMS

I

calls me her dearest her darling her daughter
kneads me between her palms until I am
small as a pomegranate seed and she can slip me
under her tongue—carry me out with her

she dawdles along behind
a stubborn child that won't even try to keep up

she brings me candles so that I can illuminate
this dark arena where my totem animal, my horse
performs its muscular battle-dance
corvettes, levades, airs above the ground

she is time after time
the destination I can't reach
an unmapped country
a gathering mist

she's caught in amber, fixed, curled tight
like the beginning of human
I wear her in this resinous tear of ages past,
hung on a silver chain around my neck

II

I'm on my grandfather's farm,
mahogany and ruby glass,
polished brass, oil lamps,
a chained dog barking.
I'm not allowed to go upstairs.
I do not go upstairs.
Mother, he says, *where's my tea?*
My grandmother

comes in from the scullery,
wiping her hands on her apron
of duty, wifely and Christian.
She lifts the teapot from the table
where he sits waiting
and pours him a mug of tea,
adds milk and stirs.
Christ is cross-stitched
into the fabric of the walls,
the unseen guest, the silent
listener to every conversation.

My mother is a scarecrow,
fixed to a hawthorn stick and stood
out in a vast field, fallow.
Crows perch on winter trees,
cattle low in the byre.
She cannot wave at me although
she knows I'm watching her
through a glass darkly.
Her ruined face is turned
towards me and into the wind.

III

All night she has rampaged around,
spoiling things and making me sad.

DEMENTED

Ha! Done it again
haven't you, left me with no
logical recourse.

It never made sense,
no: and now it never can,
(crafty old woman)

I can still argue
all I want, still it won't make
any difference

sharp as a sliver
from the magician's mirror,
an ungrateful girl.

DRIVING HOME FROM SAINTFIELD

In memory it is always raining as we are leaving.
I wave goodbye to cousins, uncle, aunt:
always past my bedtime late.

Rain knuckles the roof,
but I am snug, safe in the car's cocoon,
the blackness held outside.

The wiper's jerk and thud, the heater's blast,
curves of country roads
carrying me to the soft verges of sleep

as we move homewards
along beams of light.
My mother is singing,

The 23rd Psalm—'The Mountains of Mourne'—
'Clementine'—*Oh my darling,
oh my darling*—just for me.

LETHE

My poor mother,
for your birthday you get another 'little episode',
another transient ischaemic attack,
during which you walk into a door jamb.
Your face is bruised, as if you'd been punched
hard and when I ask if it hurts, you say
'I don't think so.' You are even more lost.
If only misery could be wiped away like memory,
like chalk marks from a board, lessons over.

My poor mother,
your bones are light as the memory of bones,
and your flesh is melted to a dream of flesh.
My heart is broken by your lightness,
by your terrible absence, as you rest
what is left against my shoulder.
I cannot help you: there is no comfort,
and this is too cruel
no matter what our sins have been.

My poor mother,
your children are un-able, for even now
your need is not greater than ours
and we have never known how.
Forgive us our trespasses
as we have forgiven your trespasses
against us. Deliver us
from this evil. Where is the river,
the beautiful, the beautiful, the river?

DAFFODILS

The Vertues.
The roots stamped with hony, helpeth them that are burned with fire.
They have also such wonderful qualities in drying,
that they consound and glew together very great wounds.

—Gerard's Herbal

I

I thought it was a fool's errand, thought
we'd never find the place,
my mother trying to navigate
with only a vague address to go by—
a farm somewhere outside Millisle.
My children bored, fighting in the back seat,
my nerves on edge, my hands too tight
on the steering wheel, stress levels high.

But we got there, loaded sackfuls of bulbs
into the car's boot, and paid the man.

For weeks afterwards, I'd look out the window
and see my mother on her knees, digging,
planting daffodils behind hedges, among trees.

II

My mother has descended into hell,
(these biblical allusions haunt me)
and daffodils are the only colour in this Easter,
yellow incongruities across the dull fields,
painfully there, like the resurrection of love.

I cut them against despair, bring
huge bundles of them into the house,
beacons burning in vases, on windowsills.

LOVE APPLES

Go past today
to where the greenhouse stands,
once upon a time.
Enter the oven of light,
where vines extend pale tendrils
and passion flowers, waxy and exotic,
tinge the scorched air with an alien scent.
Sit again on the hot brick ledge,
and watch your mother taking care
of the tomato plants: Harbingers,
Alicantes, Ailsa Craigs.

Watch the water she pours
turn into dusty bubbles,
before soaking away
down to the roots.
Thirst closes your throat.
Her finger and thumb
pinch out the side shoots
and the sap is summer seeping,
green and pungent.

Reach out your hand and pull
a tomato from its bristly stem,
feel its smooth skin,
just reddening from green
in perfect genetic memory
of ripeness, bite into the flesh
and taste its bitter sweetness,
foretaste of knowledge, banishment.

GIFTS

A missing word, a doubt.

A high shelf, a bear in the cupboard,
a mountain of books, an avalanche,
a burial on eight millimetre.

A map with all the names erased
a compass with no north, south, east or west,
a house on the fence.

Any number of untruths.

A small round pebble, cast
in flesh and lodged forever.

A maze where all the curves and passages
lead back to the beginning,
but no way in.

A clean page stained with ink,
a parable, a supposition.

PLANTER

My brother is a lean white shadow in the early morning light,
unspoken things
have kept him thin, despite his wife's attempts to fatten him on love.

From the window I watch him walk his fields to their furthest edges,
where the deer graze.
He has dug himself a place, refused to be the seed on stony ground

and with a farmer's faith, he harvests himself against winter,
each winnowing
yielding the new history that he is planting in his children' s hearts.

WORDS FROM THE OTHER SIDE

I visited my friend in hospital,
the day after she had died
and been brought back.
Her heart had stopped, exhausted
by another asthma attack,
by years of pumping
for an easy breath—
kicked back to life only
by doctors and electricity.

The air around her crackled.

Urgently
she pulled me close,
kissed my lips, placed
into the cave of my mouth,
onto my tongue
a message for me, carried back—

death's easy—she said—
much easier than life

and her words hit me
like an amphetamine rush,
dizzied me, left me
electrified, unsure
if I'd been given
a blessing or a curse.

OUTSIDE

A window looks out onto a garden
where lupins, lilies and lobelias
turn the air heady and butterflies
dip their long tongues into sweetness.

Almost hidden by profusion,
a gate opens onto a lane.

The lane wanders through hedgerows
succulent and dripping
with honeysuckle and unpicked berries,
until it disappears over a hill
and out of sight
into some other vista.

A woman stands at the window
and I imagine that she is watching
for someone, her child perhaps,
who will at any moment now
crest the hill, come into view.

When the child reaches the gate
she will go through it,
cross the grass, enter the house
and open the door to the room
where the woman stands, waiting—except—
when I move closer to the window,
shading my sight from the sun's glare
on the glass, I see only my reflection.

There is no homecoming,
only my imagining, and perhaps
I have imagined the garden also,
the gate, the lane—even the window
where no-one stands watching.

RIDDLE

As mountain
speaks to mountain and sea to sea
I hear you
and you are the voice of my loneliness
I see you
and you are a mirror held to my emptiness
I touch you
and you are the absence of love
who are you?

BAD MAGIC

It is the deepest part of the night.
An owl's fierce flight wakes the garden
from its satisfied dream of hybrid pleasure.
The lawn begins to tremble, night stock
sweats scent into the agitated air
and the fuchsia's soft fear clings to my skin
like pollen, as I move through them
to the hidden well. Carefully

I carry the severed finger he cut
from his right hand and left
under my pillow, blood
insinuating itself into my sleep,
and his voice asking over and over—
Is this what I think it is? Yes,

yes. I cast the finger over the moonlit lip
into the well's deep throat for darkness to swallow.
Now it will be *his* thirst that is never slaked
and when he rises from his own dream of restitution,
sweet water will be bitter to him: poisoned.

POETRY

I am being followed by a flock of winged words,
plagued by their black eyes and beaks.
Their tongues are sparks in the blue air
and I have heard their songs so often that I almost
understand the sense beneath the notes.
They make intricate iambic patterns round my head,
a lyric latticework, a tilt of time.
At night they roost along the window ledge
and though I've nailed my window closed,
my last waking thought is always looking for its rhyme.

THREE RING

When I am born
my family sit my plump little feet
onto the wire, so that I know its feel.
When I am four I can walk its length
with hardly a wobble. I'm in the Big Top
at seven performing without a net,
my dress hand-sequinned, my hair curled.
By ten I'm famous, known
to circus lovers everywhere.
They adore my exquisite balance—
gasping with pleasure
as I leap and pirouette
to always land steady,
my body absorbing the wire's jangle.
It is my special talent
to never think about falling.

When I'm fifteen
I marry the lion-tamer's son.
He strokes me as if I am
dangerous, enters me trembling
while the great beasts
lean against the bars, throats purring.

Gravity comes into my limbs,
and falling into my heart.

RUDIMENTARY MAGIC

The queen is counting twigs of bone, wishes
she has lined up along the window sill to dry.
The princess is playing in the barn
among the rakes and scythes and last year's hay.
The prince constructs a castle for himself,
wooden bricks piled high on the nursery floor,
keeps, turrets, dungeons. A drawbridge to raise.

A squawking makes the little princess peep
out through a knot hole in a plank
into the farmyard, where the king
is wringing a chicken's neck
with a twist of his hands.

Long seconds beating like wings
against her cheek, moving towards stillness.
Jewelled beak.
One deep red drop.
Congealing.

Soft popping of feathers
torn from skin,
soft, downy feathers, floating
like tiny insects in shafts of sun.

A cleaver's steely wink
and blood's metal clots the air.
Steaming guts, slopped
into an old iron bucket
for pigs' swill.

At dinner, the king notices his little daughter
pale, offers her slender slices of white meat
to tempt her appetite and she opens her mouth
like a baby bird, swallows.

The ruby at the queen's throat
bleeds red into the candle light
as the family proceeds,
eating down to the bones.

THE VISITOR

A December evening,
a minute before midnight,
and a bird begins to sing
from a branch in the ash tree
just outside our bedroom window.
It sings on through the night
until daybreak, its solitary trill
filling the air with sound, exotic,
notes rising and falling against the dark.

At first we are intrigued, delighted.
A nightingale? A night jar?
No ornithologists, we wonder
if it is some bird that's lost its way,
blown off migratory course
by winter storms to end up
singing at a time like this.

Then, as night after night it returns
to sing because it must,
to call a mate who never answers—
the novelty wears off.

Birdsong disturbs our sleep, our dreams
are filled with feathered longing as if
we too are being called by some thing
or some place we'll never reach now.

LULLABY

Tonight the air is thick with babies,
naked and mewing in the dark
their blind fish mouths seeking.
They float unanchored, loose in time,
ebbing and flowing with my breath
as if I am the tide of the ocean.

There is no point
in asking why they're here, they're only
babies after all, wouldn't know
what I was talking about—so—
I'll just gather shoals of them
in the nets of a remembered rhythm,
and sing myself and them to sleep.

LATELY

I've come to dread dreams, phone calls,
visitors, messages from life's borders,
for these days
it seems all the news is bad,
and though I'm scrupulous
about such assurances
as saluting magpies, throwing salt
and touching wood, it is impossible
to feel safe or immune.

I am haunted by the ghosts of old men,
and I see how time runs
past old women, how they are left
stumbling after, gasping for meaning.
Even the children are touched by fear,
become harder to comfort.

Days are so out of kilter
that I catch glimpses of the future,
but always too late to stop what happens next.

PIANO LESSON

It must have been
the sound of the piano ghost
(downstairs all alone and weeping
little silvery notes) that started me

dreaming of the woman in the bath,
letting her wrists open to the warmth,
her blood flowering in the water
like the fronds of a sea anemone

ANECDOTAL WORDS

I

She works nightshift, security, watching
the monitors, walls of glass, fragments
of city centre streets, moments of lives.
She sees all kinds of things pass by, tight knots
of drama, quick fucks in doorways, fights, tears
in the rain, drunks pissing against the wind.
Sometimes she dreams up histories, allows
these anecdotal thoughts to swell, become
stories for strangers moving through the dark—
like these two, faces lost in static snow.
Bereft of meaning or context, she gives
them hopelessness, illicit love, and ice,
a monster trapped inside a glacier,
a virus underneath the permafrost.

II

Belfast Sunday is no place for late night might-be lovers:
cold streets and closed doors, nowhere to go.
A security camera records their uncertainty,
him and her in a black and white loop, a B movie,
grainy from re-running. She's shivering
and he leans against a stone facade, holds her
as the winter wind winds her coat around them.

He's offering anecdotal evidence of warmth,
and though his words have rhythm and scansion
she knows they prove nothing, he will always be
nine-tenths hidden. Her words are a frozen weir
where a woman floats, dreaming beneath the ice.
His kisses will not warm her, nothing will melt—
there will never be anything between them but regret.

APPLYING FUZZY LOGIC

To find your own niche in love's conceptual anarchy
forget Aristotle and his either/or logic—
go for fuzzification instead: the cocaine of science.

Enter your lover's linguistic variables, his if-then rules,
his vagueness, paradoxes and information granulation
into the Kosko Fuzzy Approximation Theorem.
Make use of the machinery

for dealing with imprecision and partial truth.
The outcome will define where love stands for you
on the continuum between completely true and completely false.

This allows you a closer rapport with reality,
and can substantially increase your power.

'82-'89

It was a crooked time—

that's how it happened, that she fell for the crooked man
and went to live with him in his little crooked house
where every night she fed his crooked cat
as he counted his crooked sixpences into a purse
made from the skin of a little crooked mouse.

It was a long crooked mile back.

OUT DAMMED TEETH MARKS

next morning she finds
the distinct marks of his teeth
on her palm of all places
beneath her thumb a small bright bruise

and while she can shower
his touch from her skin
his smell from her fingers
this stigmata stays tender

a reminder
that something dangerous
has slipped its harness
but they're both sensible people really

and some days later
their sensible conversation
will use cliché
to rope it down again

drunk at the time
let's just pretend it didn't happen
then all she will have to do is wait
for the evidence to fade, be gone

the theory's fine—the difficulty is
that she is slow to mend
weeks later
a ghost trace still remains

her life's moved out of joint
as if the fates have turned
and she's begun to feel
like Lady Macbeth—indelibly stained

BITTEN

She's not at all well—
sleeplessness,
obsessive thoughts,
lack of concentration,
strange aches, dreams and cravings.

Working on the principle of homeopathy and hangovers
—treat like with like/hair of the dog—
she pours herself a drink
and wonders if he'd agree
to be prescribed for her cure:
man as medicine, labelled
take as required
until the symptoms have resolved themselves.

THE STRAW

she forgave him his trespasses,
those she knew, and those she guessed at,
so she would have found a way to forgive him
the dark-haired nurse with the coke habit—
same as the others—had it not been
for the day she came home from work
to find them both, smug
with post-coital repleteness
and just-dressedness on her new sofa
that she hadn't even got sitting down on yet herself

SHE'S TROUBLE

Saturday night,
after a few drinks,
he looks straight into her eyes,
takes her hand in his, says
she has no idea how good it feels,
asks if she doesn't love him just a little,
tempting her into compoundment
so that she goes and comes with him
so easily that she thinks maybe
she does love him—just a little.

Sunday morning,
after several cups of black coffee,
he looks sideways,
says it just doesn't feel right, besides,
he'd had too much to drink and drink
always gets him into trouble.

UNGUARDED WORDS

I've spooked myself,
indulging too freely in talk
of passion, possession,
wanting and wildness—
speaking of extremes
as if I had learnt nothing.

I am resolved
to buckle down,
adjust the harness,
get on with things,
it's not so bad, this living
in the in-between

where light and dark
are the same thing
and if a constant hunger eats
my days and nights
—so what—
it's only self: self: self.

THERAPY

Therapist 1

Once a week I see my analyst,
whose hair is black and straight
and cut severely round her face.

My analyst sits very still—an upright chair
and on the wall a plethora
of diplomas and certificates, all
authorised and signed by Freud himself.

My analyst keeps her hands neutral
and her eyes clear, although now and then
I catch a little bit of the collective unconscious,
or a dream symbol, flitting across her irises.

My analyst says very little, in fact
I remember only one proper conversation—
about the difference between milk and water
and why a man would give his son a stone
when he'd asked for bread.
Perhaps I only talk to fill the silence she has made.

Therapist 2

Has a ponytail and a white coat—
supplies me with the drug
that guarantees analgesia
whatever the pain.

He measures
on perfectly calibrated scales
a cupful of honey
that predates dissatisfaction,
decolours the combat.

See—with it
I can fold myself
into the shape of a woman.
No one would guess
I am just origami, boneless.

Therapist 3

Is Dutch,
anthroposophically trained.
To relax me, he plays cassettes
of whales singing
and his hands on my skin
are soft, slippy and slow
as ever so delicat-ely
he rebalances my *chi*.

Therapist 4

Every winter I recite my hurts
to a beautiful shaman, then
in a nightshaded dream of healing
lit by a fire's bright flicker,
he pierces my skin' s canvas with a needle of bone,
rubs charcoal of bone into the bloodless punctures
to mark every injury, illustrate my pain.

Come summer, I can read my history
in scar tissue calligraphy.

COWARD

My tongue's too smooth.
If I were braver
I would reclaim it,
impale it with surgical steel,
like a flag planted, a city retaken.

A pierced tongue
would say different things,
tell another story

but the look on your face
when I suggested it
as if I was crazy
to be even thinking
about self-mutilation.

I haven't mentioned it since.

AWAY IN THE HEAD

Returning is touch—
your fingers stitch
the ragged hole of being
into flesh, mend
the emptiness.
Skin speaks again
and through your hands
I remember
sinew, muscle, bone,
the whole substance of myself.

SMALL DEATHS

As all the years' growth engulfs my house
branches block every view of further afield,
days dawn green and dense,
light ripples like water.
My breathing slows.

Outside the window,
behind my eyes,
everything is leaf and bird
and I grow accustomed
to the habits of sparrows,
thrushes, blackbirds, finches, starlings—
their songs a thread of accidental pleasure
that skeins my heart.
Best of all I love the wrens—
but their fragility frightens me
even though I understand
a dead bird is nothing.
You could barely weigh it in your hand.

THE ART OF TYING FLIES

He's tying a Red Sedge
for those hot summer evenings
or those dead afternoons, July and August,
when he can't quite decide
what to offer the occasional riser,
close under the bank.

The body is hare's ear, spun on orange silk,
and ribbed with gold wire.
Wound all down the body from head to tail,
the hackle comes from a red cockerel.
The wings are Landrail, tied so as to lie
flat along the Sedge's back.
Beeswax the thread, wind and tie,
interweave fur and feather
until they become a living creature again,
reformed, reborn. Finished,
he holds it between his fingers,
lifts it into the light,
sees the graceful wheel of the line
as he lays it down soft as a snowflake

beautiful as any red sedge
fluttering late in the evening sun
on a slow-moving stream.

I AM

I

Today I have been a comma
between
two halves of a story.
A salmon exhausted
against the flow.

Yesterday I was silk,
I was a sweet inhalation.
I was the wood's grain.

Tonight I am the oldest woman in existence
and I have a great sorrow, a divine sorrow
that covers the face of the earth with tears.
No ark will float on it nor rainbow arch it.

Tomorrow I will be a running hare

II

I am seratonin, adrenaline,
hippocampus, synapse, nerve,
progesterone and oestrogen,
meat and juice, bone and dust.

HURT

Stay perfectly still.
Time will take this past you
if you wait. Don't struggle.

Damaged moments
flapping and circling
like great clawed birds.

Flayed hours that rattle
like gales, snow laden
from the arctic of your heart.

The questions you can't ask,
the answers you can't give,
the more you can't take—

sit it out—the nausea will pass.
Days will become linear again
and you'll resume the forward march.

BLUE

Lying awake in the vicious dark
I close my eyes and bring back blue—
holiest, calmest of colours.

I send it round my veins, flood
the empty chambers of my heart with it,
douse myself in it.

I soothe the anxious air with it,
fill my children's rooms with it,
wrap them in soft swathes of it, safe
and I can sleep
rocked in a hammock of blue
sky above, sea below.

1ST OF THE FIRST

The old year
laid down into memory
like the ring of a tree, marking
another full circle completed

and the calendar's clean days
stretching forwards,
untainted
tempt me to hope.

I am resolved
to stub out past failures,
weigh myself
on tomorrow's scales.

NOTICE OF EVICTION

You are hereby given notice
that from this day forward
your tenure has ceased.
You are therefore banned
from setting foot
in any thought process
(conscious or unconscious)
that belongs to me.

Under sub-section C
this includes dreams and fantasies
whether of a sexual nature or not.

Please note—I shall be changing the locks.

FINDING COMFORT IN FRACTALS

I imagine
applying the Mandelbrot equation
to the chaos of my life,
in putting the data of disorder,
the total randomness of it all,
thoughts and actions, desires and fears,
that change from day to day,
hour to hour, minute to minute

and finding in the end
nothing is random.
Finding beneath everything
a pattern—
beautiful as a fern, a coastline,
or the dance of planets.

ULSTER SAYS NO

Having grown up with so many given negatives
I am always and constitutionally inclined to say yes
yes let's have another drink
yes go on ahead
yes of course you can
yes I'll try that
yes why not?
yes have some of mine
even when it might be more prudent to decline.

STILL

I have stuffed my mouth with silence
gagged myself with an iron will
my throat choked
on questions

but I still ache
for the one perfect word

I have bound myself to uncertainty
staked myself to not knowing
against the siren song
of absolutes

but I still long
for the whole spirit of the law

I have sought out darkness
gone down the ways of the night
invited my nemesis
into my house

but I still crave
the green pastures

moss on a stone
long grass in the rain

where I could lie down
beside the still waters

time floating
clear and effortless

and wake restored

IF I ASKED YOU TO

would you set down your drink,
get up from your seat
and dance me, waltz me
across this chequered floor, unclamp me
from the crocodile jaws of tedium
lift me, defy my gravity, whirl me
away from black and white
and shades of grey,
de-compose me to all the colours,
balance me on your fingertips
a rainbow arc, promise me,
delight me with delicacy, undo me,
help me out of my head
into the honeycomb of flesh
until I am sticky with sweetness: fill me.

POSTCARD FROM THE ISLAND OF LIZARDS

I am salamander in the all day sun
among almonds and pomegranates.
As mornings liquefy to afternoons

I grow sweet and satisfied,
soaking light, warming bones.
A great turtle holds up the earth,

little salty fish leap to my dish
and thirst is a cool spring.
Nights I sleep in a white house

where Mary Mother of God
gazes on me with love. P.S.
dreams have returned.

CESAR MANRIQUE

You used an island
for your canvas,
flourished in a desert home
of unremitting hardness
by finding out hollows,
spaces where air held back
molten rock, created
a place to live and grow
like lichen, a new beginning.
You tempted the wind with toys,
listened to the music
that stone offered to your ear,
deep magic of caves,
beauty in paucity,
metamorphosis in fire.

My small daughter christens you
our man Reeki
catching my feeling
that you and I
are on the same side.

WORDS FROM THE PAST

A man from far away
has brought a gift you must accept
for he has crossed all the world's borders,
travelled through places you can only imagine,
to bring it to you, icy tundra in his eyes,
the wind howling your name.

You must invite him in,
take what he gives
no matter what it is,
a white lily or a millstone,
a letter fallen from the pages of a book
you lift at random from the shelf.
A book you have not read for years,
communication from a previous life.

PEARL DIVING

Leaving the air behind
I go down
body slicing
layers of filtered light
shoals of small distracting fish
to bulging darkness

slow
      slower

deep
      deeper

until it does not matter
if I never rise again
into the bright clamour
of living and sun

but rising always comes

gathered in my hands
tight shells to be prised
opened to find
the preciousness of pain

THE PRODIGAL DAUGHTER

That woman—the one who left the house
to buy a pint of milk, and then just disappeared—
has been found again, living on a beach,
identified. Despite the pleas
of family and friends, she declines
all offers of a ticket home and will not tell
the four year story of her anonymity.

She shuns the fifteen-minute bribes
of newspapers and magazines,
preferring to remain balanced on her toes,
a ballerina on a jewellery box,
the mirror sea beneath.

She keeps her words there;
recites them to the holy blue of sky
and hears them back on tongues of birds,
sees their little tongues flicker
beneath the eggshells,
birthing an oratorio of wings.

GEOGRAPHY

I dream of maps
laid out across my table,
across my years, with little flags to mark
where such and such a thing happened,
pinpointing
which road was taken,
when and where the choice was made that led
to this particular configuration
of hills and valleys, the topography of now.

MACGILLYCUDDY REEKS

I cannot find these mountains on my map, in fact
I'm starting to think that they're not mountains at all—
just the ghosts of mountains
who have not understood that their aeon has past.

I DO NOT

I do not confess to anything—so when I speak
of the small dark spidery creature
skittling across the periphery of my vision—
it proves nothing.
Meaning is just an accident,
soon mopped up—those letters
were written by someone else,
and that suitcase under the bed
does not contain my heart.

I do not regret anything—so when the black dog
digs up the bones I have buried
beneath the brambles, deep in the wild woods—
I am not worried.
I have allowed no prophets
to enter my house, so bones can not
stand up, grow flesh and walk.
They cast no shadows
and I have nothing to look in the face.

I do not promise anything—so when I lie
down with you, close as a child,
intimate as a lover, tender as a mother—
it means nothing.
Love is just a trick of the light,
a misunderstanding.
No matter who you think I am,
when it matters most,
I will not be who you want.

GONE

There's nothing to me—
see how I have already
slipped through your fingers,
a conjurer's trick.
an empty gesture
you are left with.